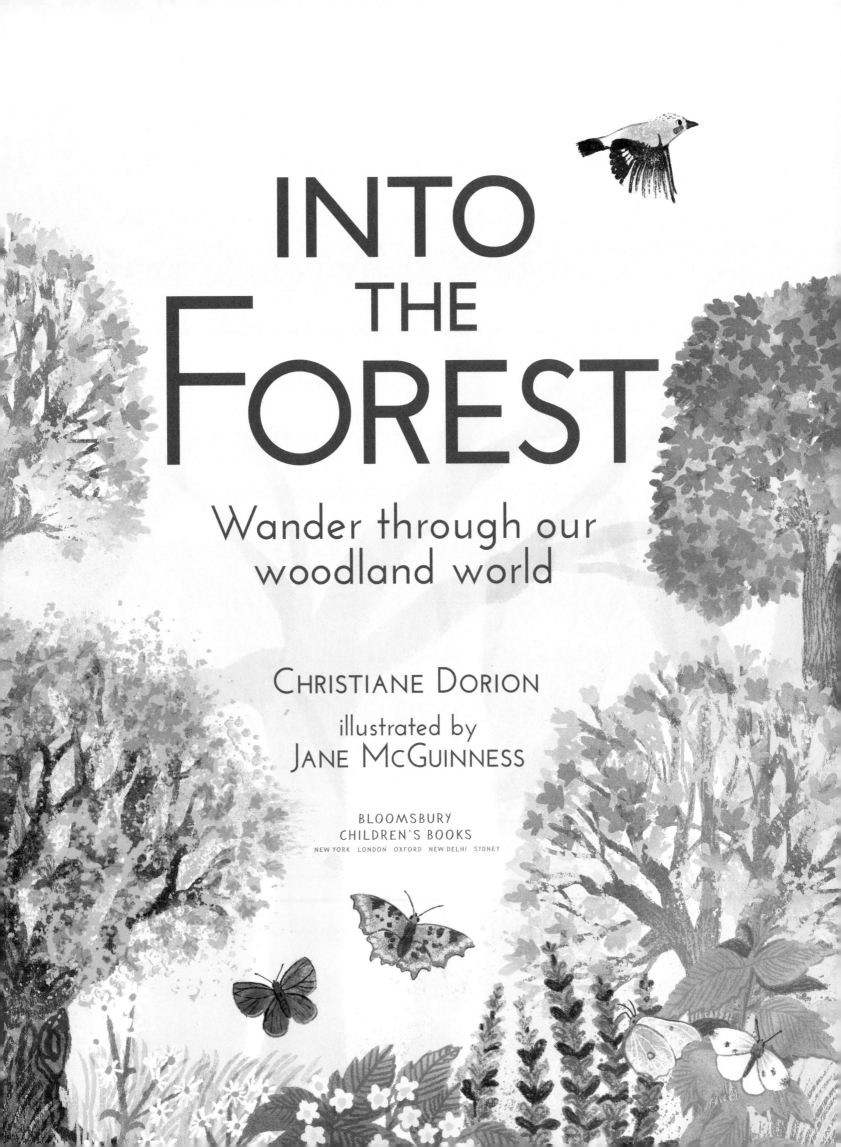

INTO THE FOREST

Wander through our woodland world

CHRISTIANE DORION

illustrated by
JANE McGUINNESS

BLOOMSBURY
CHILDREN'S BOOKS
NEW YORK   LONDON   OXFORD   NEW DELHI   SYDNEY

For Geneviève, Timothé, and Archie —C. D.
For Rich and Comet, who share my woodland walks —J. M.

Contents

North
AMERICA

equator

South
AMERICA

Forests of the world

Forests are wonderful places to explore, from the vast expanses of evergreen trees in the north to the hot, steamy jungles along the equator. They vary depending on where they grow on the planet and how much sunlight and water they receive. Take a stroll through some of the main forests of the world and meet the many extraordinary creatures that live in them.

EUROPE

ASIA

AFRICA

AUSTRALIA

Coniferous forest

Deciduous forest

Tropical rainforest

From seed to tree

Imagine entering a dense forest. A picture of tall trees and dark shadows may come to mind. But forests are home to a rich variety of plants, animals, fungi, and tiny creatures that all interact with each other and their surroundings to survive. Every tree in the forest is a world teeming with life.

wood pigeon

great spotted woodpecker

The life of a tree

Small seed

Like most plants, a tree starts as a small seed buried in the ground. Inside the seed, a mini plant is hidden, with its own supply of food to help it to grow. The seed can stay dormant in the soil for days, weeks, or even years.

Green shoot

When there is enough warmth and water, the seed opens and the tiny plant starts to grow. A root anchors it in the soil and a small shoot pushes up toward the sky.

Seedling

The first leaves unfold, fresh and green, and the plant becomes a seedling. Already it faces many dangers, from being eaten by a hungry rabbit to being uprooted by strong winds or crushed under the wheels of a tractor.

Sapling

With a bit of luck, the plant continues to grow and grow to form a sapling. It grows for years, standing in all weather, getting bigger and bigger, until it matures into a strong, beautiful tree.

Fully grown

After many years the tree is old enough to produce flowers. These flowers contain a special dust called pollen. The powdery pollen drifts with the wind or is moved by bees, birds, and other creatures to mix with, or pollinate, the flowers of another tree. When pollinated, these flowers slowly turn into fruits that contain and protect the precious seeds. The fruits can fall down to the ground, get blown by the wind, or be carried by animals away from the parent tree, to where there is more space and light. And when the conditions are just right, the seeds might open and new trees start to grow.

Little helpers

Birds and other animals help spread the seeds of trees. They often bury them for the winter when food is harder to find. Many seeds are forgotten in their secret places and some grow into new trees.

jay

An oak tree can produce up to 50,000 acorns in one year, but only a few will grow into trees.

7

Leaves, trunks, and roots

Like all living things, trees need food to stay alive, grow, and thrive. Animals can move around to look for leaves and juicy berries or to hunt other creatures, but trees and other plants are rooted firmly to the ground. They produce their own food, using sunlight, carbon dioxide from the air, and water from the ground.

Food for all

Insects, rabbits, voles, and many other animals feed on plants. Animals such as owls and foxes eat other animals. When living things die, they are a feast for earthworms and many other tiny creatures that live in the soil.

robin

The leaves

Leaves are like mini food factories powered by the sun. They absorb sunlight and carbon dioxide from the air to help the tree make its own food. In the process, leaves give out oxygen, which is essential to all animals on Earth. This process is called photosynthesis.

roe deer

blue tit

tawny owl

The trunk

The woody trunk, tall and strong, supports the tree and its heavy branches. It also contains special cells that carry water and food to different parts of the plant. The tough bark protects the tree from invading insects and bad weather.

The roots

The long roots spread wide into the ground and hold the tree in place. They also collect water and nutrients from the soil, needed for the tree to grow, and store it as food for the plant.

9

From tree to forest

When trees grow strong and tall, their branches, full of leaves, begin to form a dense canopy. Like a huge umbrella, the trees provide cover for shade-loving plants to grow on the forest floor. As trees grow and new plants take root, the woodland slowly turns into a magnificent forest.

New life

When an old tree dies and falls to the ground, it creates a clearing. The decaying wood provides food and hiding places for armies of small crawling creatures. New seedlings take advantage of the light, and delicate flowers that only bloom in the sun can now grow on the forest floor.

Colors and scents

The flowers' bright colors and fragrant scents attract butterflies that come to sip their sweet nectar. Fluttering their wings, butterflies carry pollen from one flower to another.

comma butterfly

Many animals come to the forest for food and shelter. After they feed on berries and nuts, they scatter plant seeds in their droppings and help the woodland spread and flourish. Also, the breeze blows new seeds to the area, some attached to fluffy parachutes, others with papery wings that spiral down like tiny helicopters. Some of these air-blown seeds might one day find the ideal spot to take root.

In the trees

The whole forest is alive with birds chirping loudly in the trees, acrobatic squirrels scuttling along branches, and bees buzzing through the air.

red squirrel

On the lookout for food

A spider is busy spinning its intricate web, waiting patiently for a fly to come along. But it had better watch out! Not far away, hungry birds are on the lookout for a crunchy spider.

treecreeper

Bats shelter in tree trunks.

The cooing call and clatter of wings of wood pigeons can be heard in the forest.

nuthatch

hedgehog

The forest floor

On the forest floor, small creatures snuffle, crawl, or hop under the thick carpet of fallen leaves in search of food and a safe place to shelter.

Deciduous forests

Forests vary depending on where they grow on the planet. Deciduous forests are found in places where there is plenty of rain and four distinct seasons through the year. Summer, autumn, winter, and spring come and go, and plants and animals have to adapt to the changes.

badger

Each level of the forest is home to a rich variety of creatures, large and small. Birds gather twigs, moss, and grass to build their nests high up in the tree branches, while bats roost in the holes in tree trunks. The thick undergrowth offers cover for grazing animals such as rabbits and deer. The roots of trees provide solid structures for badgers to dig their burrows under.

Summer

In the summer, the sun is bright, the days are long, and the trees are full of green leaves soaking up the light. Each leaf contains a chemical called chlorophyll. This enables the leaf to make food from sunlight and gives it its green color.

A tree through the seasons

Most trees in the deciduous forest have broad, flat leaves that capture plenty of sunlight during the warm summer months and fall to the ground before the winter arrives to save water and energy. Heaps of dead leaves gather on the forest floor, breaking down slowly to make the soil richer for new plants to thrive.

Autumn

As the days get shorter and cooler in the autumn, trees sense the changing light and their leaves stop producing chlorophyll. Their green color fades away and other colors take over, creating a fiery display of red, orange, and gold. Then the leaves fall to the ground.

Winter

Like sleeping giants, deciduous trees stay dormant over the cold winter. Their branches are bare. The forest is still and crisp, as snow slowly and softly tumbles down.

Spring

When the weather turns warmer and the days get brighter and longer, new buds appear and fresh green leaves grow in the trees. Another year in the forest begins.

15

Hidey-holes and safe dens

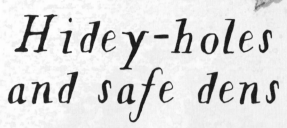

Like trees, woodland animals have to adapt to the changing seasons in the deciduous forest. In the warm summer, they enjoy plenty of food and places to hide. As chilly weather creeps in, food becomes harder to find. Some animals store nuts for the cold months ahead, while others enter a long winter sleep. Many birds fly to warmer places to escape the cold, but some stay for the winter, fluffing up their feathers to keep warm.

Hibernation

Hedgehogs, dormice, and bats fatten up for the cold months ahead and find shelter for their long winter sleep, called hibernation. Their heartbeat slows down and their body temperature drops to save energy. These animals can survive for months without food.

Dormice hibernate for up to seven months.

Safe shelter

A hollow plant stem or small crevices in tree bark are fine places for ladybugs and other insects to hide from the cold.

Food storage

Squirrels collect and store nuts to get ready for winter. They bury the nuts in the ground and, when needed, use their amazing sense of smell to retrieve their stash of food.

A hidden world

Snails and slugs leave a slimy trail as they search for plants to eat.

stag beetle

common toad

While some creatures make their home high up in the trees, others prefer the damp, dark forest floor. Fallen leaves and branches shelter an abundance of small creatures, from shiny beetles to slimy slugs, snails, and shy toads.

The decaying leaves and crumbling wood are a feast for earthworms, beetles, fungi, and many creatures too tiny to be seen. All these living things play an important role in the forest. They slowly chew up dead matter and enrich the soil for new plants to grow.

Logs and stumps

The many nooks and crannies of old logs and tree stumps are safe places for insects to lay their eggs and shelter from the cold. Birds, toads, and other animals come here to hunt for food.

19

A walk in the woods

The forest changes throughout the year, and a walk in the woods brings many different sights, sounds, secrets, and surprises.

A summer day brings amazing sights and sounds.

Birds sing in the treetops.

A bumblebee buzzes.

An autumn day brings a fiery display of colors.

Autumn leaves glow red, orange, and gold.

leaf skeleton

Helicopter seeds fall from the sky.

bright red toadstools

Butterflies sip the nectar of flowers.

A frog croaks on the forest floor.

Blackberries shine on prickly brambles.

A winter day brings frosty new textures and shapes.

A spring day brings new growth and life.

A spiderweb sparkles in the bright winter sun.

catkins in the trees

Bare, crooked branches make beautiful silhouettes.

Soft buds can be seen on smooth twigs.

a bird's nest

A dormouse wakes up after a long sleep.

sweet chestnuts with a prickly shell

Blue, yellow, and white flowers carpet the ground.

21

Deciduous trees to spot

Deciduous trees grow in different shapes and sizes. Some have a broad crown of leaves, while others are tall and slender. Looking at the shape of the tree and its leaves helps identify it.

common hawthorn

common alder

sycamore

elder

littleleaf linden

aspen

common beech

blackthorn

wych elm

English elm

22

common hazel

horse chestnut
(conker tree)

sweet chestnut

rowan
(mountain ash)

hornbeam

field maple

common ash

sessile oak

English oak

silver birch

23

Clark's nutcracker

moose

great blue heron

Cape May warbler

snowshoe hare

Coniferous forests

The world's largest coniferous forests stretch across the northern hemisphere and are known as boreal forests. As the weather changes from season to season, plants and animals adapt from short, mild summers to long and bitterly cold winters. Evergreen trees stand tall and straight, close to one another, like an army of soldiers reaching for the sky. A thick bed of moss covers the forest floor, and few plants grow in the dark shade of the trees.

The land is sprinkled with lakes, rivers, and streams carved by glaciers thousands of years ago. In summer, large swarms of mosquitoes, blackflies, and other insects hang over the water, attracting many birds. Lots of forest creatures come to the river to drink and find food.

Beavers cut down trees to build a dam across the river, altering the forest.

wolf

25

Cones and needles

Most trees in the coniferous forest are evergreens with needle-like leaves. In the long winter months, the days are short, the ground is frozen, and there is little sunlight and water. To withstand the cold and make the most of the light, these trees keep their leaves all year, shedding them a few at a time instead of all at once.

Needles

Conifers have very thin, sharp leaves, or needles. Their dark color and waxy surface help to absorb light and hold on to water in the freezing weather.

black-capped chickadee

Cones

Instead of growing flowers, conifers grow cones to make their seeds. The seeds form when pollen is blown by the wind from a male cone to a female one. Over time, the cones ripen and, when the weather is warm and dry, they open to release their seeds. These glide through the air with their tiny wings to find a suitable place to sprout.

Sharp teeth

A red squirrel bites the cones with its sharp teeth and gnaws its way through to the seeds, leaving piles of stripped scales on the ground. Squirrels collect and store cones to eat during the winter. Some of these cones get forgotten, and the seeds can grow into new trees.

Finding food in the coniferous forest is not easy, especially in the winter when the ground is buried under thick snow. Squirrels and some birds have clever ways of extracting the tasty seeds deep inside the cones. Meanwhile, they help trees by spreading their seeds across the forest.

Special beaks

The red crossbill has a curious beak, with crossed, curved tips. To open the tight cones, the bird inserts and twists its bill between the scales and pulls the seeds out with its tongue.

Seed stashes

The Clark's nutcracker uses its long, sharp bill to chisel open the cones and extract the nourishing seeds. This small bird can carry stashes of seeds in an expandable pouch under its tongue and hide them across the forest.

red crossbill

Acrobatic birds

The small chickadee hangs upside down on a cone to pick at the seeds with its short, pointed bill. It gathers seeds in crevices of tree bark to eat later. Its "chick-a-dee" call brightens up the winter woods.

Clark's nutcracker

boreal chickadee

27

Beneath the trees

The forest floor is dark and gloomy, and very little light filters through the tall trees. A thick mat of moss covers the ground, soaking up the rain. On the wet and soggy soil, fallen leaves and twigs break down very slowly. In some northern forests, the soil beneath the surface is frozen all year round. In others, it covers a deep layer of rock. Tree roots are shallow and few plants grow in these harsh conditions.

magnolia warbler

woodland caribou

Silvery lichen

Lichen grows well on tree bark and rocks and is a good source of food for caribou, moose, and other animals. It is also a handy material for birds and small mammals to use to build their nests. Lichen may look like a plant but it is formed of a fungus and tiny algae that benefit from growing together. The fungus provides shelter and collects water, while the algae make food from sunlight.

Spongy moss

Large clumps of green moss cover the forest floor. Unlike other plants, mosses don't produce seeds, flowers, or cones. Instead, they make new plants by releasing millions of tiny spores that spread with the wind, like fine dust.

Feathery ferns

Ferns also grow on the moist, shady ground, slowly unfurling their feathery leaves. Like mosses, they reproduce using spores, not seeds. These are hidden inside small brown dots under their leaves.

Carnivorous plants

In the shady bogs and marshes of the forest, where the soil is poorer, some plants get food by luring insects into deadly traps. The pitcher plant attracts its prey into a pool of liquid inside its large, rolled leaves that look like flowers.

Mysterious fungi

Neither plant nor animal, fungi thrive on the dark, damp forest floor. They help break down dead trees and other plants, slowly turning them into soil. Fungi are a feast for many forest animals, from chipmunks to voles and black bears. These picky eaters know which ones are safe to eat!

chipmunk

29

ermine

spruce grouse

Silent winter

When the cold winter arrives, there is little sign of life in the forest. The ground is covered with a heavy blanket of snow, lakes turn to ice, and a bitterly cold wind whips through the trees. Few animals live here all year round, but those that do have thick layers of fur or feathers to keep them warm. A glimpse of white fur behind a tree might be a snowshoe hare or an ermine, with a winter coat that blends in with the white snow. Sharp claws help some animals climb up trees to find shelter, while large paws and hooves help others walk on the snow without sinking too deeply. The forest is still, as many birds have flown to warmer places.

Animals search for shelter in the cold, snowy forest.

Canada jay

three-toed woodpecker

The **tap tap tap** of the woodpecker making holes in the trees echoes throughout the woods. Small birds find shelter in the holes, their heads tucked under their fluffy feathers. Animals are hard to spot, but their footprints can be seen in fresh snow as they roam the forest in search of food and a safe place to hide.

Many birds migrate to warmer lands, but some stay here all year round.

snowshoe hare

31

Winter homes

With freezing weather and very little food around, many forest animals find shelter for the long winter. Some look for a dark, quiet place to sleep through the coldest months. Others use the thick blanket of snow to shield themselves from the weather and to hide from hungry predators. The animals spend the winter surviving and waiting for warmer days and plentiful food to return.

Resting bears

When the weather turns cold and food is scarce, bears know it is time for their long winter rest. In fall, they eat and eat all day long, to build up a thick layer of fat, then find a dark cave or tree hollow to make their den. When winter arrives, they enter their burrow, curl up into a big furry ball, and settle into a deep sleep. Female bears give birth to their cubs in the den and emerge with them in the spring.

brown bear

Many forest animals hibernate during the winter.

Chipmunks

Chipmunks shelter in underground burrows beneath the trees. They curl into a small ball to keep warm and go to sleep, waking up every few days to feed on their hidden stash of seeds.

Little brown bats

Little brown bats huddle together in dark, damp caves and hibernate through the winter.

Frozen frog

In the coldest months, the wood frog buries itself under leaves and freezes. Its heartbeat and breathing stop and it turns to ice. When spring arrives, the frog thaws and comes back to life.

Ruffed grouse

In very cold weather, the ruffed grouse takes a big plunge into the fluffy snow, flaps its wings to make a deep hole, and disappears for the night. The bird uses its body heat to stay warm. When morning comes, the grouse flaps its way out of the snow and takes off.

Voles and foxes

Voles remain active through the winter. To keep warm, they dig tunnels under the snow where they forage for roots and seeds close to the ground. These little critters have to be on their guard when they emerge from their burrows, as hungry foxes might be watching.

Green giants

Coniferous forests don't grow just in the far north; they are also found in milder climates, from high mountains to rainy coasts. On the west coast of North America, where the ocean brings plenty of rain in the winter and fog in the summer, one type of forest is home to the tallest and widest trees on Earth. Large redwood conifers soar into the sky like towering giants, protecting each other from the wind and collecting moisture from the fog through their leaves. Some of the majestic trees hidden in these forests have lived for more than two thousand years.

Roosevelt elk

A bald eagle flies high up in the sky.

The thick bark of redwood trees shields them from bugs, disease, and fire.

Coniferous trees to spot

Coniferous trees grow tall, straight, and close to one another. Many are shaped like a triangle so they can shed heavy snow in the winter.

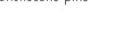

bristlecone pine

balsam fir

black spruce

jack pine

American larch

Scots pine

Norway spruce

white spruce

Douglas fir

European larch

western red cedar

white pine

giant sequoia

coast redwood

blue-and-yellow macaw

spider monkey

two-toed sloth

tree boa

Beautiful
butterflies flutter
about.

Rainforest
animals come
in a rainbow
of colors.

Tropical rainforests

Tropical rainforests are filled with colors, sounds, and textures. These forests are found near the equator, where it is hot and humid all year round, with plenty of sunshine and rain. The trees grow tall and close together, draped in climbing plants and brilliant flowers, all racing to reach the sunlight. Most trees are evergreen and their leafy branches spread out to form a wide canopy, capturing much of the rain and casting shade on the forest floor.

Below the canopy grow smaller shrubs and young saplings waiting for an old tree to fall so they can catch the light and flourish. Each layer of the forest harbors many extraordinary animals, from large tarantulas crawling on the ground to sleepy sloths hanging in the tree canopy and solitary eagles perched on the tallest treetops.

harpy eagle

capuchin monkey

scarlet macaw

Rich variety of life

More than half of the known plants and animals in the world are found in rainforests, and many more are yet to be discovered.

A noisy place

Most creatures of the rainforest live in the tree canopy, where there is an abundance of food and places to shelter. The rain slowly drips down through the trees and collects inside leaves, forming pools of water where birds and small animals come to drink. Bees and butterflies sip the sweet nectar of flowers and spread their pollen through the forest. Monkeys leap from tree to tree using their long limbs and gripping tails to move around. Many animals make loud noises to tell each other where they are in the dense tangle of leaves and branches. Screeching macaws, croaking frogs, and howling monkeys make a deafening jungle chorus.

SQUAWK

Climbing plants

Climbing plants attach themselves to trees with tiny hooks and wind their way up toward the sunlight.

Loud monkeys

The howler monkey has the loudest voice of the forest. Its powerful call warns other animals to stay well away from its patch of woods.

HOWL

coati

Fruit and nuts

Many trees produce their seeds inside juicy fruit or hard shells. Birds, monkeys, and other animals feast on the fruit and nuts, helping to spread seeds across the forest in their droppings.

keel-billed toucan

Delicate orchids

Beautiful orchids sprout high up in the trees to reach the light. They anchor their small roots on branches and take water from the steamy air.

Some animals don't make any noise at all.

Hanging lianas

Lianas hang from one tree to another, creating useful paths for animals to move across the forest.

DRIP DRIP DRIP

A silent sloth

A silent sloth hangs upside down from a branch, holding on with its long curved claws, fast asleep most of the day. Feeding on leaves, fruit, and twigs, this curious animal rarely touches the forest floor. Green algae grow on its thick fur, helping it to blend in with the forest.

Long journey up

Poison dart frogs lay their eggs on the moist forest floor. When the tadpoles emerge, they wriggle onto their parents' backs to travel all the way up to the tree canopy. The adults drop their precious broods into a pool of rainwater inside a leaf. When the tadpoles grow into frogs, they climb down to the forest floor.

Green waxy leaves

A rich variety of trees and lush green plants fill the dense canopy. Their leaves are broad to capture the sunlight, with a waxy, shiny surface and pointed tips to shed heavy rain.

Bold macaws

Noisy, colorful scarlet macaws feed among the branches of tall trees, using their strong beaks to crack open nuts and seeds. Messy eaters, they drop many on the ground, helping new plants to grow.

Hanging nests

Oropendolas weave their nests with long, narrow leaves, attaching them to the tips of branches away from unwanted visitors. These birds often pick branches close to wasps' nests to keep their chicks safe, as hungry predators tend to stay away from stinging wasps.

Bright feathers and cozy nests

Of all the forests in the world, rainforests have the richest diversity of birds. Most live here all year round, but some come to visit from faraway lands to escape the cold. The tree canopy is filled with bright toucans, parrots, and hummingbirds creating bursts of color as they fly through the forest. The wealth of fruit, nuts, flowers, and insects in the trees makes a feast for the birds. High branches and hollows in tree trunks are good places to build their nests. With just a beak and claws for tools, the birds turn twigs, leaves, and mud into intricate, cozy nests to lay their eggs and raise their chicks in.

Warm homes

Harpy eagles gather sticks and branches to build their large nests in the tallest treetops. It can get windy up there, and to keep their chicks warm, the eagles line their nests with leaves, feathers, and soft animal fur.

Beautiful birds brighten the rainforest with colors.

Flowers and nectar

A hummingbird hovers above the flowers, beating its tiny wings so fast that it makes a humming sound. With its long, thin bill, it reaches deep inside a flower to sip the nectar. As it flies around the forest, the hummingbird carries pollen from one flower to another.

Sweet treats

A toco toucan can reach ripe fruit on the thinnest branches with its huge, bold beak.

The dark forest floor

The forest floor is dark and damp, as little sunlight passes through the trees above. Fallen leaves, fruit, and twigs are quickly broken down by worms and fungi. The soil is shallow, and large tangled roots rise above the ground to anchor the tallest trees. Although the forest seems still, countless insects scuttle around, looking for food among the leaves and tree roots. Holes in the ground are secret entrances to the hidden nests of spiders, ants, and other crawling creatures. Small animals roam the shady forest floor in search of food.

Foraging about

A small agouti forages quietly for insects, roots, and fallen fruit on the ground, fearful of being heard by a hungry jaguar or other predators.

Watch out!

The poisonous bushmaster lies curled up on the forest floor, waiting for a small animal to pass by. Its brown markings hide it well among the dead leaves on the ground.

Busy ants

A procession of leafcutter ants are busy carrying small pieces of leaves back to their underground nest. The ants grow a fungus garden on the pile of leaves to feed the whole colony.

Hercules beetle

giant centipede

Eight legs hiding

A large, hairy tarantula hides in its burrow, ready to pounce on a crunchy insect or a hopping frog.

Colorful frogs

Tiny poison dart frogs flash their bright colors to warn other animals they are poisonous and not good to eat.

45

A rainy place

The rainforest is a rainy place. The air is hot and steamy, and short, sudden bursts of heavy rain fall on the forest almost every day. The rain trickles down slowly through the dense canopy, soaking the forest floor. The trees take plenty of water from the ground and lose plenty of water through their leaves. As the steamy air rises and cools, thick clouds form above the forest and it rains again. Water also collects in streams and rivers meandering toward the ocean, creating giant cascades of white water and often flooding the forest. Flowering plants and tall grasses grow along the rivers, making the best of the sunlight.

A falling raindrop can take ten minutes to travel from the canopy to the forest floor.

Amazon kingfisher

Expert diver

Silently, a kingfisher dives headfirst into the river without a splash and returns to its perch with a fish in its beak.

Teeming with life

Rivers and streams are teeming with fish of all shapes and sizes, providing food for many animals.

Resting time

A sleepy jaguar lies on a low branch near the river in the dappled shade of the forest.

Colors and camouflage

The rainforest is full of color, from the fiery shades of tropical flowers to the bright feathers of birds and dazzling butterflies fluttering their wings in the sun. But when there is danger, some animals become invisible. Some pretend to be a leaf or a twig, while others stay still to blend in with their surroundings.

emerald tree boa

white-throated toucan

Potoo

The curious-looking potoo rests upright on a tree stump, with its beak pointed toward the sky, looking like an old branch.

turnip-tailed gecko

Horned frog

The horned frog, well hidden on the forest floor, can easily be mistaken for an old wrinkled leaf.

Blue morpho butterfly

The blue morpho butterfly produces flashes of vibrant blue as it flies through the forest. When it lands on a leaf and folds its wings, the butterfly turns brown and seems to vanish.

Animals such as the green iguana have colors that perfectly match their surroundings.

Stick insects

As they stay perfectly still, some insects pretend to be a leaf or a twig to trick predators.

katydid

praying mantis

spectacled owl

red-eyed tree frog

Many animals
are awake
at night.

jaguar

The moon peeks through the many leaves and trees.

kinkajou

potoo

giant cane toad

Night in the forest

As day turns to night, the forest becomes a different world. Many animals come down to the forest floor to hunt, their beady eyes glowing in the dark. Small bats unfold their leathery wings and glide between the trees for a mid-flight feast of tasty insects. They listen to the echoes of their own sounds to navigate their way in the darkness. The spectacled owl hunts on silent wings for a small rodent on the ground, while the potoo scans the forest with its bright yellow eyes to find insects to eat. A tree frog shoots its long sticky tongue out to catch a moth. The jaguar with its beautiful dappled coat uses its keen sight and hearing to hunt quietly on the forest floor. In the dark forest, it is hard to tell the hunter from the hunted.

Tropical trees to spot

Tropical rainforests are home to the widest variety of trees of all the types of forests. Most trees grow tall, with long, thin trunks and branches spreading wide to capture the light. Many trees produce tasty fruit and nuts.

palm tree

cinnamon tree

cacao tree

wild cashew tree

açaí palm

avocado tree

walking palm

balsa tree

mango tree

kapok tree

Brazil nut tree

rubber tree

chicle tree

mahogany

53

Energy from the sun

Plants capture energy from the sun to make their own food. Animals feed on plants and, in turn, are a source of food for other animals.

Dusted in pollen

When bees and butterflies feed on flowers, they move pollen from one flower to another. Plants use this pollen to make their seeds so that new plants can grow.

Scattering seeds

Many plants produce their seeds inside tasty fruit. Birds and other animals feed on the fruit and help to spread the seeds.

song thrush

Working together

All living things in the forest play an important part, from the largest trees to the tiniest insects. They all depend on each other and their surroundings to form a vibrant ecosystem.

Fungi and trees

Fungi come in many shapes, colors, and sizes and help to keep the forest healthy. They break down the remains of plants and animals and put goodness back into the soil.

oyster mushroom

beefsteak fungus

turkeytail fungus

fly agaric toadstool

Trees and fungi help each other to thrive in the forest. Tiny fungi grow around tree roots and spread their fine threads far and wide under the ground. The fungi suck up water and minerals for the tree. In return, the tree provides food for the fungi.

Underground

When wriggly worms and small mammals tunnel through the ground in search of food, they let air and water in and turn the soil, helping new plants to grow.

A small patch of soil is home to millions of living things, many waiting to be discovered. Tiny creatures, too small to be seen, nibble on dead leaves and bits of wood to make the soil rich and crumbly.

All elements of the forest are important.

What forests do for the planet

Forests play an important role for wildlife, people, and the whole planet. They are home to a rich diversity of plants and animals, as well as millions of people who depend on them for their livelihoods. Many things we need in our everyday lives come from trees and other plants, from the air we breathe to the food we eat.

A place to live and work

Forests provide a home and work to millions of people around the world.

Capturing water

During heavy downpours, trees in forests catch much of the rain through their leaves, allowing it to trickle down slowly into the ground. Trees also release water back into the air from their leaves. Clouds form and it rains again.

A haven for wildlife

Forests are home to countless species of plants, animals, and other living things.

Natural resources

Trees provide us with valuable resources such as wood for timber and paper.

Protecting
the soil

Tree roots absorb water like big sponges and help to hold the soil together.

Fresh air

Forests are the air conditioning system of our planet. They soak up carbon dioxide from the air, helping to keep the planet cool. Meanwhile, they give out the oxygen we need to breathe.

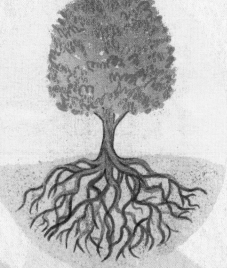

Healing
plants

Forests contain amazing plants with the power to heal.

Places to
enjoy

And there is something magical about exploring and being in a forest.

In some parts of the world, forests are specially grown to produce the resources we need. But in other places, vast areas of natural forest are lost every year for timber and to make way for farmland, roads, and more homes. It is important to use and look after our forests wisely and in a sustainable way so they can continue to support life—plants, animals, and us—now and in the future, forever.

A source of food

Forests give us food, from fruit, seeds, and tree sap to edible fungi and wild animals.

How to plant a tree

Create a new home for wildlife by planting a tree! Find a good spot and ask permission. It could be in your yard, around your school, or in a local park. Then choose a tree that is suitable for the site, making sure that it has enough space to grow and the right type of soil and amount of sunlight.

1. Dig a hole

Dig a hole slightly wider and deeper than the tree's roots.

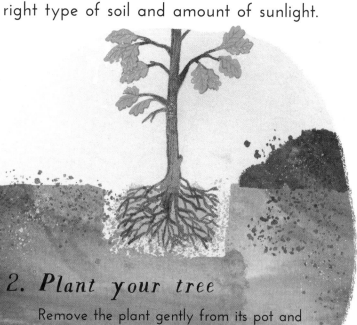

2. Plant your tree

Remove the plant gently from its pot and place it in the hole. Make sure the base of the trunk is level with the top of the soil.

3. Put the soil back

Hold the tree upright and fill around the plant with soil without leaving any air pockets. Make sure your tree is steady.

4. Support your tree

You can cover your tree with a guard if necessary. Using a stake provides extra support.

5. Your tree adapts

Trees adapt to the natural conditions where you plant them, so watering shouldn't be necessary. If the weather is particularly dry, you may water your tree thoroughly.

With time, your seedling will grow into a strong, beautiful tree and provide food and shelter to many insects, birds, and other animals.

To grow your own tree, you can even collect seeds in the autumn, like squirrels do.

Tell everyone why we need to protect our forests and trees!

Forest animals

Can you find these animals in the book?

fox

wood pigeon

roe deer

blue tit

hedgehog

great spotted woodpecker

purple hairstreak butterfly

moose

great blue heron

snowshoe hare

bald eagle

dormouse

blue morpho butterfly

chipmunk

common toad

red squirrel

boreal chickadee

red crossbill

scarlet macaw

green iguana

potoo

Hercules beetle

two-toed sloth

capuchin monkey

white-throated toucan

red-eyed tree frog

hummingbird

Glossary

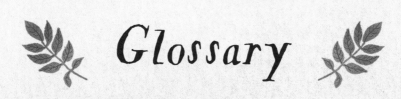

boreal forest a type of forest that grows in cold areas, formed mainly of evergreen trees; also called taiga, boreal forests make up a third of the world's forests

camouflage colors and patterns that help an animal hide or blend in with its surroundings

canopy the thick layer of branches and leaves in a forest

carbon dioxide gas made of carbon and oxygen, absorbed and used by plants to make food and released by animals when they breathe out

catkin a cluster of tiny flowers growing on certain trees

cell the smallest part of a living thing

chlorophyll the pigment that gives plants their green color and enables them to make food from sunlight

conifer evergreen tree that has needle-like leaves and cones, such as a pine or fir

decaying breaking down slowly or rotting

deciduous a tree that loses its leaves once a year, usually in the autumn, such as an oak or beech

ecosystem plants, animals, fungi, and bacteria that live together in a particular environment, interacting with each other and their surroundings

evergreen a plant that remains green throughout the year

fungus type of living thing that is not a plant or an animal

hibernation when animals slow their body activities for a period of time so that they seem to be in a deep sleep

nectar sweet liquid inside flowers that is food for animals

nutrient a substance needed by living things to grow and survive

photosynthesis the process plants use to make their own food (sugars) out of water, carbon dioxide, and sunlight

pollen a fine dust made by flowers that allows plants to make seeds

pollinate to carry pollen from one flowering plant to another to allow that plant to produce seeds

predator an animal that hunts other animals for food

sapling a young tree

sustainable a way that we can keep using natural resources for a long time without running out, for everyone now and in the future

There's lots of information online about the most up-to-date
efforts to conserve forests around the world.
Here are a few websites to check out.

The National Forest Foundation: nationalforests.org
Arbor Day Foundation: arborday.org
Rainforest Trust: rainforesttrust.org
Woodland Trust: woodlandtrust.org.uk

BLOOMSBURY CHILDREN'S BOOKS
Bloomsbury Publishing Inc., part of Bloomsbury Publishing Plc
1385 Broadway, New York, NY 10018

BLOOMSBURY, BLOOMSBURY CHILDREN'S BOOKS, and the Diana logo
are trademarks of Bloomsbury Publishing Plc

First published in Great Britain in November 2019 by Bloomsbury Publishing Plc
Published in the United States of America in November 2020
by Bloomsbury Children's Books

Bloomsbury books may be purchased for business or promotional use. For information on bulk purchases please contact
Macmillan Corporate and Premium Sales Department at specialmarkets@macmillan.com

Library of Congress Cataloging-in-Publication Data
available upon request
ISBN 978-1-5476-0457-9 (hardcover)

Printed and bound in China by Leo Paper Products, Heshan, Guangdong
2 4 6 8 10 9 7 5 3 1

All papers used by Bloomsbury Publishing Plc are natural, recyclable products
made from wood grown in well-managed forests. The manufacturing processes
conform to the environmental regulations of the country of origin.

To find out more about our authors and books visit www.bloomsbury.com and sign up for our newsletters